The Gift of Knowing *you*

Discovering
the Power
of Your Story

Joselyn Smith-Greene

Neroli Tree Press
Glen Oaks, New York

Copyright © 2020 by Joselyn Smith-Greene
First Edition
All rights reserved.
No part of this publication may be reproduced, distributed, or transmitted in any form or by any means, including photocopying, recording, or other electronic or mechanical methods, without the prior written permission of the publisher, except in the case of brief quotations embodied in critical reviews and certain other noncommercial uses permitted by copyright law. For permission requests, write to the publisher, addressed "Attention: Permissions Coordinator," at the address below.

Neroli Tree Press
PO Box 40263
Glen Oaks, New York 11004
NeroliTreePress.com

Ordering Information:
Quantity Sales. Special discounts are available on quantity purchases to corporations, professional associations, and others. For details, contact publisher at address above or email info@joselynsmithgreene.com.

Editing by Marla Markman
Interior Book Design by Kelly Cleary
YOUr Story Kit Illustrations ©2019 Evan Greene

Publisher's Cataloging-in-Publication Data:
(Prepared by The Donohue Group, Inc.)

Names: Smith-Greene, Joselyn, author.
Title: The gift of knowing you : discovering the power of your story / Joselyn Smith-Greene.
Description: First edition. | Glen Oaks, New York : Neroli Tree Press, [2021]
Identifiers: ISBN 9781734020403 (print) | ISBN 9781734020410 (ebook)
Subjects: LCSH: Self-actualization (Psychology) in women. | Self-realization in women. | Women--Life skills guides.
Classification: LCC BF724.65.S44 S658 2021 (print) | LCC BF724.65.S44 (ebook) | DDC 158.1082--dc23

ISBN Print: 978-1-7340204-0-3
ISBN E-Readers: 978-1-7340204-1-0

Library of Congress Control Number: 2019920593
Printed in the United States of America

Following the advice in this book could transform your life. On the other hand, after reading the book and engaging in the journey process, you may not find yourself any better off. The content is my personal experience, expression, and opinions. You are responsible for your own choices, actions, and results. Use your best judgment. Neither the publisher nor I shall be liable for any physical, psychological, emotional, financial, or commercial damages, including, but not limited to, special, incidental, consequential, or other damages.

*To my husband, Glen, and my sons,
Justin and Evan, who are deserving of my best.*

CONTENTS

❁

Dear Reader • vii

1
Preparing for the Journey • 1

2
Who Are You? • 9

3
What's Your Story? • 17

4
Are You Afraid to Be Alone? • 29

5
What Is Your "It"? How Do You Find It? • 37

6
How Do You Want to Show Up to the World? • 57

7
How Do You Continue the Journey? • 71

8
Transforming Darkness into Light • 93

Dear Gift Recipient • 99

"
The internal critic often quickly ruins self-esteem, developed after some reckless and painful word claimed from some factor in our past, and the scoreboard maintains a tally of the triviality that sustains such a declaration!

—James Nussbaumer

Dear Reader,

When I was 8 years old, one day while helping me with my homework, my father said, "You don't know the answer? What are you, stupid?" One mean-spirited rhetorical question altered the trajectory of who I was supposed to be and how I valued myself. It is my earliest memory of where my downward spiral of insecurity, self-doubt, and emotional turmoil began. But it also served as the foundation for my resilience, the reason I developed my internal cheerleader voice, and the basis for my self-love and the self-care I practice today.

While questions can be disruptive, they can also be the vehicle for personal discovery that allows the truth of who we are to surface so we can evolve. By asking myself questions, I was able to view my story through various lenses, helping me understand the bigger picture, heal my emotional wounds, and transition into a place of forgiveness, appreciation, and contentment. My answers enabled me to create a life rooted in thankfulness, with an appreciation and reverence for life's tiniest moments. The process required my stillness, focus, and the tenacity to reverse the rage. Questions are powerful; they can open doors to our destined greatness.

The questions presented in this book are a springboard for you, the reader, to begin examining your story through different lenses. The acknowledgment of all our experiences, our backstory, can add value to our lives and serve as inspiration to others. Inspiring you to reflect on who you are and what truly matters is my gift to you.

Love and Blessings,
Joselyn

"
There is no greater gift
you can give or receive
than to honor your calling.
It's why you were born.
And how you become most
truly alive.

—Oprah Winfrey

CHAPTER 1

Preparing for the Journey

The greatest gift you can receive is the knowledge of who you are. *The Gift of Knowing You* is intended to spark the realization of your truest essence, giving you clarity on what makes you who you are, unlike no other. Discovering how you see yourself, recognizing your personal greatness, and realizing your life purpose are the objectives of this journey. The only requirement for you to receive this priceless gift is your willingness to dwell within.

In this book, I will guide you through a creative process of discovering who you are from the inside out. You'll recognize what captivates your attention and why. The questions scattered throughout the book are intended to spark internal dialogue as you travel along your discovery journey. You will also find creative play and exploration activities. Creative self-discovery is not about making stuff; rather it's about finding a mode of self-expression that speaks to you. It's listening to your inner voice. It's getting lost in the doing. It's about providing food for your soul and creating the pathway to your authentic self.

The "we" in the pages that follow refers to you and me because I'm on a journey right alongside you. To help you navigate more easily, I share parts of my personal journey thus far. Keep in mind, life journeys are ongoing, a continuum, an evolution, and a testament to a fulfilled life.

Before we embark, let's consider three important factors that will help maximize a successful journey. The first is mindfulness. Mindfulness is being present with your thoughts and feelings, while being aware of what's going on around you. It's the ability to stay focused on what you are doing as you are doing it, independent of your life circumstances. Past hurts, worries, and responsibilities are kept at bay as you process each moment. The past is the past, and the future is yet to be. The present moment is the equalizer that levels the playing field. Regardless of economic status or the level of success achieved, the present moment is all any of us truly have.

Perhaps mindfulness can be better understood by providing a few examples of what it is not. It's not completing your morning routine and later wondering, "Did I ... ?" (fill in the blank with any of your morning tasks). It's not getting to your destination and wondering how you got there. It's not formulating your response while another person is still talking. It's not replaying past moments or anticipating future ones.

Instead, mindfulness is disengaging from autopilot and bringing your awareness to what is unfolding before your eyes in real time. Bringing your awareness to the present moment is the easy part. Staying in the present moment can be quite arduous, as there are so many distractions vying for your attention. How you remain in the present moment is an individual strategy that can develop over time. Exercise 1, at the end of this chapter, offers suggestions to help you begin flexing your mindfulness muscle.

The second factor is self-awareness. According to Merriam Webster, self-awareness is "an awareness of one's own personality or individuality." Collectively, your personality, emotions, strengths, weaknesses, beliefs and motivations comprise your individuality. When attuned to each of these areas, you are in the best position to understand who you are and operate in a way that serves you. You know exactly what you are thinking, what you are feeling, and most important, you know why.

The foundation of self-awareness rests on your ability to be vulnerable and examine your experiences. This might be difficult. It might involve reliving a painful part of your life. Although it's challenging to reflect on unpleasant experiences objectively, they can offer great insight into who you are today. The more you connect the dots between the past and present, the more self-aware you become.

Another important factor of self-awareness is being aware of the impact your words and actions have on others. In real time, you are cognizant of their facial expressions, verbal responses, and body language. These observational cues can offer insight into the quality of your interactions and the degree to which you are received.

Our ability to self-assess and self-monitor lessens the chance of knee-jerk reactions. Reactionary responses, behaviors, and unexplained emotions can cause distress, uneasiness, and inner turmoil. It can allow unsettling and unproductive thoughts to run rampant. With self-awareness, you are operating from a place of mental clarity, giving yourself the headspace to navigate life with intention. Self-awareness is like a muscle. To strengthen the muscle requires mindfulness and honest self-assessment. The more you exercise it, the stronger it will become.

The third factor that will help you along your journey lies in your ability to question yourself. Questions are powerful. They encourage thought and reflection. As you question yourself, be mindful and aware of your reactions and how you respond. Your responses to the questions in this book can provide you with your roadmap for living your authentic life.

Like questions, quotes are powerful too. They help solidify an understanding capable of leaving an indelible imprint on your mind and, even more important, a lasting impression on your soul. I have included quotes throughout the book to inspire and encourage you to be on the lookout for other meaningful quotes as you travel along your journey.

With mindfulness, self-awareness and self-reflective questions, the process of self-discovery is easier. You are in the best position to identify what's important, what matters, and your unique recipe for harvesting your joy. As you grow and evolve, your recipe for joy will likely morph and change as well. As you strengthen your connection to "self," you will also find that ordinary moments become extraordinary. Are you ready to begin your gifted journey of discovery? Let's start with the first of three major questions: Who are you?

PREPARING FOR THE JOURNEY

> Self-awareness is our capacity to stand apart from ourselves and examine our thinking, our motives, our history, our scripts, our actions, and our habits and tendencies.

—Stephen Covey

EXERCISE 1

FLEXING YOUR MINDFULNESS MUSCLE

One of the best ways to begin exercising your mindfulness muscle is to turn off your autopilot. Here are a few suggestions that will help you reinforce your connection to the present moment:

- Brush your teeth or write with your nondominant hand.
- Change the order in which you put on your clothes.
- Take a new/different route than you normally would to your next destination.
- Count how many different smells or sounds you encounter on your next walk.
- Acknowledge and document any daily experiences that make you smile.
- Consider keeping a mindfulness journal centering on a goal you want to achieve. Schedule a few minutes in your day to write a short entry that focuses on your reflective thoughts, progress, and feelings as you work toward your goal.

Switching up your usual routines will help you to stay focused on what you're doing moment to moment.

> Mindfulness isn't difficult. What's difficult is to remember to be mindful.

—John Teasdale, Research Scientist

> At the center of your being you have the answer; you know who you are, and you know what you want.

—Lao Tzu

CHAPTER 2

WHO ARE YOU?

*I*f you were asked, "Who are you?" would you be able to respond without referencing family title, marital status, job title, life responsibilities, gender, ethnicity, religious affiliation, or any other common descriptor? What would you do in lieu of family, career, and financial and life responsibilities? Shop till you drop, travel, volunteer? And after you tire of retail therapy and traveling the world, then what? Not sure? Guess what? You're not alone.

It's easy to get attached to our job titles and life roles. Think about when we're out socializing. Our name, connection to the host, and vocation are the usual conversation starters, as in the following example:

> "Hi, my name is Eileen. I'm Barbara's sister."
> "Hello, I'm Adrienne, nice to meet you. Barbara talks about you all the time. You live in New York, right?"
> "Yes, I'm a stay-at-home mom of two boys who keep me busy 24/7. How about yourself?"
> "Barbara and I used to work together."

> "Oh, are you a teacher?"
> "Not anymore. I left the classroom to take on an administrative role. I have two children. My son is a junior, and my daughter is a senior in high school. Hard to believe my husband and I will soon be empty nesters."

Without realizing, we place ourselves in neat little boxes and categories so that the rest of the world instantly knows who we are. When we do this, we stifle, limit, and lose sight of the most unique and interesting parts of ourselves. Not only do we lose, but the world loses too.

When our everyday tasks don't align with who we are, we disengage. Autopilot kicks in. Life becomes blurred, and we lose sight of the importance of each present moment, one by one. Unfulfilled moments turn into unfulfilled hours. Unfulfilled hours turn into unfulfilled days. Unfulfilled days turn into unfulfilled years. Our connection to our self erodes. We might accomplish a lot, but it doesn't necessarily resonate with our soul.

What are some indications that you've lost that connection? Your responsibilities have turned into mindless routines rather than welcomed opportunities. You feel as though you're existing rather than thriving, or a piece of your puzzle is missing. Knowing who you are and what inspires you has become a distant memory. A part of you lies dormant, yearning for something more. And for some, it's possible the puzzle was never completed; the connection was never made and will need to be discovered for the first time. If you're experiencing any of the above, a discovery process is in order to eliminate the void. Your unique specialness is waiting to be discovered or rediscovered by you.

Think about what is important to you, what you want to bring to the world, and the impact you wish to make. How do you want the world to be different because of your existence? What is your unique something that you, and only you, can offer? Where do you find joy? Exploration, growth, and evolution are paramount to establishing and maintaining a personal connection with our self. Celebrating who we are and nurturing our unique qualities every day are requirements for personal restoration. Unsure what that extra special something is? Welcome to the first major stop on your self-discovery journey.

Connecting with What Makes You Uniquely You

The qualities that make you unique are the greatness within you. But sometimes our greatness gets dismissed or devalued. Other times, our greatness gets buried, untapped, or ignored, and we must work to bring it to the surface. Gifting yourself your full attention allows you to develop a relationship with your inner self, giving you the opportunity to identify the special qualities that make you who you are.

The conversation between Eileen and Adrienne at the beginning of the chapter would be quite different if the exchange moved away from their life responsibilities and focused more on how they self-express and connect to who they are by engaging in activities they love. It would sound more like this:

> "Hi, my name is Eileen. I am Barbara's sister."
>
> "Hello, I'm Adrienne, nice to meet you. Barbara talks about you all the time. You live in New York, right?"
>
> "Yes, I do. What a fabulous top you're wearing. The color palette is so beautiful. Would you mind if I snapped a pic? I would love to add it to my inspiration wall."
>
> "That's right, you paint. With all the inspiration you probably encounter walking the streets of New York, I am honored that my top inspires you. I was in New York not too long ago, and I was mesmerized by everything. I went to the Museum of Art and Design. Blown away. I didn't want to leave."
>
> "Oh, that's my favorite museum!"
>
> "I'm including it in a piece I'm writing."
>
> "You're a writer?"
>
> "Yes, my urge to write was a natural extension from my journaling practice. Journaling opened me to all these story ideas swirling around in my

head. I felt this unrelenting push to explore those ideas and do something with them. I'm attending my first writers' group next week. I can use the feedback and desperately need to be in the company of other writers."

"That's so wonderful! But how do you find the time to write with your demanding job?"

"I squeeze it in as best I can. I think about content ideas while I'm commuting to and from work. Sometimes I research plot settings during my lunch hour. That way, when I sit down in the evenings to write, it just flows."

"Nice."

"And what's your secret, Ms. Stay-at-Home-Mom? How do you find the time to paint with your two active boys?"

"Well, I've tried a lot of things, but what works best for me is waking up before everyone else. The house is quiet, I'm rested, and, like magic, the paintbrush just dances along the canvas."

"Well, I am just going to have to check you out on Etsy."

"And I look forward to reading your book one day."

"I'm going to be in town for a couple more days. Have any suggestions for creative places to visit?"

Did you notice that the conversation now revolves around activities, like painting, writing, and exploring? When you move beyond the day-to-day responsibilities and talk about what inspires and motivates you—what makes you uniquely you—it sparks a very different conversation and allows us to connect on a deeper level. Next time you're out socializing, how about initiating a different conversation? What topics can you discuss other than the usual conversation starters, like in the first exchange in this chapter? Think about what inspires you. Maybe it was something you read or an experience you connected to deeply that changed your perspective on life. Or perhaps you started a new hobby or activity or just achieved a goal. Challenge yourself to go beyond the usual surface talk.

We can nurture our relationship to self by stepping away from our familiar life roles and embrace the uncertainty of new experiences. Whether it's elevating our conversations, entering a competition, taking a class or attending a talk outside the realm of our usual interests, or organizing a gathering around a shared interest, we can spread our wings and explore and create new ways of being. Remaining mindful of our thoughts and feelings as we navigate through these uncharted territories, we gift ourselves the opportunity to gain additional insight into who we are.

EXERCISE 2

ROLE AND RESPONSIBILITY ASSESSMENT

Think about your present-day responsibilities, activities, and tasks. As you engage in your life activities, do your best to be present with how and what you are feeling and whether it elevates you. Do you look forward to some and resent others? It might be helpful to write them down along with a brief comment about how each one makes you feel. If you're a numbers person, consider rating each responsibility with respect to the personal satisfaction you experience carrying out each role on a scale of 1 to 5, with 5 being most satisfying and 1 the least satisfying. If you dislike certain aspects of your job or family life, be honest. The purpose of this exercise is to begin extracting accurate clues about how your present-day validates (4s and 5s) or detracts (1s and 2s) from who you are.

You can download a "Role and Responsibility Assessment" worksheet at https://joselynsmithgreene.com/book-downloads.

> You can't really know where you are going until you know where you have been.

—Maya Angelou

CHAPTER 3

WHAT'S YOUR STORY?

After you assessed your life responsibilities by completing Exercise 2 in Chapter 2, you likely gained insight into what aligns with who you are and what doesn't. How about life in general? Do you look forward to each day, or do you feel like you're just doing time? Even when everything is falling in place and you're achieving your life goals (e.g., graduation, job, marriage, children, promotion, homeownership, entrepreneurship), you might still feel a residue of emptiness lingering inside. A range of reasons could be to blame, but sometimes it's because your backstory affects your present story. To benefit and learn from your backstory and understand where you are now, you need to be mindful of where you've been. This is something I know about all too well, because once I allowed my backstory to overshadow my joy.

Backstory Reflections

I was in my late 20s when I began reflecting on my backstory. I was sick and tired of feeling and reliving the emotional upset that occurred at the mere mention of my father's name or by being in his presence. My father was a stranger to me.

As I mentioned previously, my earliest memory of the discord between my father and I occurred when I was around 8 years old. He was helping me with my homework. When we came to a question I was unable to answer, my father's response was: "You don't know the answer? What are you, stupid?" The tears welled in my eyes, and my young brain soaked up his comment like a sponge. I spent years trying to prove him wrong and convincing myself that I was worthy of his esteem.

My father was kind to the outside world and abusive to his immediate family, yet brilliant at maintaining the facade of a happy family. Abandoned by his mother, he was raised by a foster mother who was physically and emotionally abusive. My father's unresolved pain and anger prevented him from achieving any sense of normalcy as a parent. He had the innate ability to poke at my insecurities—to make me feel ugly and less than. It was an uphill battle as I struggled to deal with the emotional abuse. I desperately wanted and needed him to be my cheerleader, but it wasn't until much later that I realized he was incapable of this.

I feared my father. I can't remember a time when his presence didn't trigger an unpleasant visceral reaction; my stomach would clench and my chest would tighten immediately in his company. You never knew what would set him off. One day, when my father came home from work, he became enraged because the bedroom I shared with my sister was a mess. Yelling at the top of his lungs, he slapped his hand so hard on the desk that when he lifted his hand, it was covered in blood. It was that kind of constant insanity and misplaced aggression that rocked my young world.

His belittling and inappropriate remarks continued to fuel my insecurities. It was exhausting trying to figure him out or develop enough armor to shield against his unkind words. As I grew older, his presence began to incite disgust and anger in me. It hurt too much to be around him, and I began to count down the years when I could escape to college.

The Mother Who Couldn't See

In addition to the tumultuous relationship with my father, I didn't feel like my mother was in my corner, either. Even though she witnessed his sharp tongue, she would tell me not to upset myself. How could I not be upset? How was I supposed to dismiss his hurtful words? She didn't see or realize the effect they were having on me. I started to suppress my feelings, and the rage inside me was often unbearable.

When my mother went back to school to pursue her graduate degree and worked full time after graduation, I was overburdened caring for my younger brother and assuming the household responsibilities. While my friends were socializing and participating in after-school activities, I was running home to take care of him. If my brother wasn't fed and his homework completed by the time my mother arrived home, it was a major problem. By the time I finished attending to him and cleaning up the dinner dishes, it would be very late. I stayed up into the wee hours trying to complete homework assignments and keep up with my studies. I often operated on three to four hours of sleep. My home responsibilities coupled with my learning challenges made life difficult. To my dismay, I allowed my mediocre grades and standardized test scores to define me. No matter how hard I tried, my efforts never translated into the grades I wanted to achieve or deserved. It was a constant blow to my self-esteem. I felt defeated, angry, and alone.

Living in an unhappy home, saddled with way too much responsibility and no release or means to decompress compromised my health. The constant angst kept my stomach tied in knots. The result was many trips to the doctor and a litany of medical tests. At one point, I was diagnosed with colitis and prescribed mild tranquilizers. I took them, but they didn't provide the relief I desperately needed. No medication could repair the emotional pain I was suffering. At one of my lowest points, in desperation to stop the pain, I swallowed a handful of the pills, hoping not to wake up. But I did.

The Road to Healing

It took me years to unravel, dissect, and understand the emotional trauma I endured. I was tired of feeling rage when I thought about my childhood. I knew I had to deal with the pain, address my brokenness, and work on forgiveness. I journaled my way through a lot of the hurt, read self-help books, and practiced the spiritual healing practices like forgiveness and self-care presented on *The Oprah Winfrey Show*. Collectively those three things saved me. There will always be reminders or triggers that cause the pain to surface. The word "stupid" always makes my stomach clench. My reaction is a conditioned response.

> And the day came when the risk to remain tight in a bud was more painful than the risk it took to blossom.

—Anaïs Nin

But with mindfulness, I can acknowledge the discomfort, then let it go. The work to remain whole never ends.

Not too long before his death, I could sense my father coming around. Perhaps it was a sign of his self-reflection and self-forgiveness coming to light. As foreign as it was to hear, he would utter words of encouragement in my direction, but it was too little too late. After spending my childhood watching him empower and cheer on others while desperately trying to be the source of his esteem, his kind words fell upon deaf ears. I had already begun perfecting the craft of being my own cheerleader to survive the rage and emotional rollercoaster I had been on for so long.

I continued journaling and making peace with my broken past. I wanted to be better, not just for myself but for my children as well. I have been truthful with my children about my childhood struggles and unhealthy relationship with my father. I wanted them to know that darkness doesn't have to last forever; light is inevitable if we allow it in. It is only when forgiveness reigns that your heart can begin to heal.

Journaling encouraged self-reflection and self-awareness, opening the door to realizing and understanding my emotions. You become aware of what's important, what matters, and what you value. You realize your strengths and your weaknesses and what motivates you. You get to the heart of who you are, strengthening the connection to your inner self. What I love most is that self-reflection affords me the headspace for my creativity and thought processes to soar without limits.

A Revelation

When I reached adulthood, I realized your personal best is all that matters. What I know now is that every individual blossoms in their own way and time. For me, it was during my graduate studies at New York University. Married, expecting my first child, working full time, and taking a full course load, my plate was full. Finally, my grades reflected my efforts. My graduation was one of the most defining and affirming experiences in my life, a true indication and measure of who I am. I was never so proud to walk the line with my first-born son in tow. I was my own victor.

My graduation from NYU was the first one that my father attended. He conveniently went missing for my high school and college graduations. Looking back, his absence was for the best, as it gave me the opportunity to enjoy those milestones without upset or pretense.

The irony of my educational challenges is that my father struggled in school too. I didn't find that out until after his death. When I perused his college transcripts, I was in disbelief. Had he been able to reconcile his own tumultuous childhood and come to terms with his own backstory, perhaps it could have made the difference in our relationship and eased my struggles as well.

Peace Starts Within

What matters most is how we reconcile unpleasant life experiences. We can choose to allow the pain to consume us and lead us down a self-destructive path, to lash out at others, and/or rob ourselves of a purpose-driven life.

Or we can transform our pain and make a better life for ourselves, our loved ones, and the world. Choosing to ignore or wallow in our misery will leave us vulnerable to self-medicating with drugs, alcohol, food, gambling, shopping, hoarding, or any other activity that offers us a temporary escape. Choosing to acknowledge and deal with the pain requires self-care, self-love, and forgiveness. Finding a way to reconcile destructive thought processes, whether it's from professional help, spiritual guidance, or simply putting pen to paper, is a conscious decision. As uncomfortable as it may be, it's necessary to feel and acknowledge the pain in order to ascend out of our darkness, heal, and use our experiences in service to others.

I wish my father's emotional abuse wasn't part of my story. But it is. At the beginning of my healing, I realized I had to make a choice. I could allow it to eat me up and remain bitter. Or I could use it to fuel my transformation. Today, I affirm, "I'm worthy and I matter," even when I'm not feeling it—in fact, especially when I'm not feeling it. I know hope and faith will see me through. I know what I need to do to get me through life's not-so-great moments. By doing all the above, I was able to redirect my journey.

Stepping Stones to Transformation

The purpose of Exercise 3 at the end of the chapter is to help you uncover the elements of your personal backstory. It is our backstories that make us unique. Because of my own struggles in school, I have devoted a significant amount of time volunteering in both my sons' schools. I felt compelled to be a voice for "underperforming" students and initiate dialogue about self-esteem whenever possible. All students deserve to feel good about themselves regardless of their academic abilities. This connection between my backstory and my volunteer efforts is a perfect example of how to use painful experiences as stepping stones to serve others.

Perhaps you have heard Oprah profess her love for her fourth-grade teacher, Ms. Duncan. She had a tremendous impact on Oprah. Ms. Duncan instilled confidence in Oprah, making her feel she could take on the world and igniting a spark of lifelong learning. Oprah channeled her confidence, inspiration, and desire to teach into an iconic talk show—and became the teacher she always wanted to be. *The Oprah Winfrey Show*, and later the OWN network, has provided Oprah with the platform to educate viewers all over the world.

Singer and songwriter Christina Aguilera has been forthcoming with her childhood experiences. She grew up with a father who abused her mother. Witnessing the abuse left her feeling powerless and afraid. Her backstory is why Christina vows never to be financially dependent on a man and why she is proactive and vocal about domestic violence issues today.

Acknowledging, processing, and using our story is an important part of our journey. It requires us to self-reflect and evaluate all our life experiences. That means that we should not only recognize our "defining moments," but also make peace with the hurt or disappointments we have suffered and any obstacles we have encountered as well.

EXERCISE 3

SELF-REFLECTIVE THOUGHT PROMPTS

Your reflections are an opportunity to identify your defining moments, what you think is important, and what has had a great impact on your life. They are also the stepping stones to discovering who you are. Write a journal entry for the following questions about your childhood and early adult years:

- What's the hardest thing you ever had to do?
- What are you most proud of?
- What's your greatest accomplishment?
- What's an experience that changed you?
- What broke your heart?
- What's your greatest obsession?
- What's the hardest thing you have endured?
- What achievement showed you what you are capable of?
- What's the most important lesson you learned?
- What are your strengths and weaknesses?
- Who's your best friend and why?
- What's your favorite memory?
- What's your worst memory?

You can download the above "Self-Reflective Thought Prompts" at https://joselynsmithgreene.com/book-downloads.

> The greatest gift that you can give yourself is a little bit of your own attention.

—Anthony J. D'Angelo, Author

"
Some steps need to be taken alone. It's the only way to really figure out where you need to go and who you need to be. Alone time is when I distance myself from the voices of the world so I can hear my own.

—Oprah Winfrey

CHAPTER 4

ARE YOU AFRAID TO BE ALONE?

There are many benefits to spending time alone. Undistracted alone time gives your brain the opportunity to decompress and reset, providing the mental clarity to engage in deep thought and reflection. You become more creative and productive. You put yourself in the best position to gain insight into who you are, what you want, and the direction you wish to take.

How do you feel about being alone? Do you always find yourself in the company of others? Does eating alone at a restaurant frighten you or seem like an uncomfortably awkward thing to do? Can you take a long walk alone without being plugged into music or conversation? A woman once confided in me that she was terrified of being alone in her own house. I was stunned by such an admission, and although I never found out why, it struck me deeply and I was saddened by her uneasiness. After all, our homes should be our refuge, offering renewal, restoration, and peace.

Get Comfortable with Being Alone

Uninterrupted alone time, free of distractions, provides the headspace to sort through our story. So, why is being alone so scary? When we are alone, we become more conscious of the voice within chattering away. Thoughts we work hard to suppress rise to the forefront. Maybe there's pain, sorrow, or regret we want to avoid. Distracting ourselves from our unresolved thoughts and/or issues resides in fear—the fear to confront, accept, and embrace our truest self. If you can relate to this, how about kicking fear to the curb and gifting yourself your full attention to allow your inner voice to surface? Throw away the negative chatter, concentrate on the positive, and document your thoughts as they are valuable clues in your self-discovery journey.

If being alone makes you uneasy, take baby steps and ease into it. At home, think of it as a party for one. Make it fun. Put on your favorite music and dance like nobody's watching and sing like nobody's listening. Even if it's for a couple of hours, pretend you're free as a bird with nobody to answer to.

As for dining out alone, if it feels strange, allow yourself to get lost in a book as you enjoy your meal. Or you can bring a pen and paper and see what fills your page. Look around and observe and appreciate your food and surroundings. Jot down whatever comes to mind. What are your thoughts? How do you feel? What catches your eye? Why? Or if you love to write, pen a poem or write a short story. No pressure—it doesn't have to be some magnificent piece of work. It just needs to come from you; an expression of who you are. Your alone time is your opportunity to connect with the inner you. There is one rule when going solo: electronic devices are allowed only if you are using them to play relaxing music or guided meditations. Being distracted by social media, games, or update notifications will defeat the purpose of your alone time and prevent you from the very thing you are trying to accomplish—discovery from within.

Finding your alone time might require some finagling, given your family, work, and personal obligations. It might mean getting up in the morning before your family or staying up late after everyone else has gone to sleep. It might mean leaving your home and finding a quiet place elsewhere.

As you get more comfortable with being alone, you can slowly delve into quiet, reflective activities. Try the following:

- Use journal prompts to examine specific areas of your life.
- Create a personal manifesto that outlines your core beliefs, what you stand for, and how you wish to live your life.
- Write a letter to your younger self, including any regrets, missed opportunities, and what you could have done differently.
- Try meditation, yoga, or walking on a trail.

Engaging in activities that require you to look within will elevate your self-awareness abilities and allow you to know yourself better.

> Knowing how to be solitary is central to the art of loving. When we can be alone, we can be with others without using them as a means of escape.

—Bell Hooks (Gloria Jean Watkins),
  Author and Feminist

Just to recap, alone time at home doesn't mean binge-watching your favorite show or being distracted by social media or surfing the internet. Instead, it is an opportunity to reflect, decompress, and exercise self-care. If your time is spent wisely, your alone time will move you toward your highest self.

Find Your Own Little Corner

A designated personal place in your home to be alone with your thoughts will enable you to more easily embrace your discovery or rediscovery journey. Think about the lyrics to the song "In My Own Little Corner" from *Cinderella*. While sitting in her own little corner, in her own little chair, Cinderella dreams of being a young Egyptian princess or a milkmaid or a mermaid dancing upon the sea, allowing her mind the freedom to dream with no boundaries.

If you have an entire room to yourself, that's a true blessing. But even if you have to create a nook in a corner of a room, repurpose a walk-in closet or, like Cinderella, designate a chair to retreat to in order to seek and gain the clarity everyone deserves to have in their lives, be sure to take full advantage of your dedicated space. Your personal space is your designated spot to go to think, de-stress, dream, journal, read, meditate, or whatever you find relaxing. Surround yourself with special things that offer comfort. A journal, pen, and candle, while sitting in my comfy bedroom chair, are all I need to tap into the inner me. Immediately, I transition into a place of simple joy that is peaceful and soothing to my soul.

If a nook or corner space is out of the question, a pretty basket, box, or tote filled with inspiring ephemera is a portable alternative you can use anywhere, inside or outside your home. Fill your container with meaningful remnants of your life—for example, memorable photos, awards, correspondence, reminders of an accomplishment, travel mementos, motivational items, quotes, etc. Anything that brings a smile to your face belongs in your personal space or grab-and-go container.

Singer and actress Janelle Monae practices meditation and self-care, and asks herself self-awareness questions to stay grounded. When traveling, she packs family photos to ease loneliness on the road, and brings a candle to make herself feel at home, as well as an inspirational collage she made of her favorite performers to keep herself motivated.

Setting the Stage for Growth

Once you've carved out some alone time and have a designated space to relax and process your thoughts to focus on your personal restoration, the next step will likely be reinforcing the habit of retreating to your space. A 2009 study conducted on 96 participants by the University of London found that it took, on average, 66 days to develop a habit. Regardless of where you may fall on the habit formation timeline, consistently putting yourself first and making the concentrated effort to schedule uninterrupted alone time is key. Creating the headspace to develop your self-awareness sensibilities is the precursor to gaining clarity about who you are.

EXERCISE 4

CLAIMING YOUR PERSONAL SPACE

Survey your home and identify a space you can make your own. Clear away any clutter so you can start with a blank canvas. Look for inspiration online that is similar to your space for inviting and transformational ideas that appeal to you. Challenge yourself to use what you have to transform your space into what you want it to be. In the end, you are creating an inviting and restorative space where you look forward to spending time alone.

" Dancing for me is my oxygen. You have to find something that allows you to live and breathe, no matter what's going on in your life. You have to have something to go to.

—Dwana Smallwood, former Alvin Ailey Dancer, Founder of the Dwana Smallwood Performing Arts Center

CHAPTER 5

What Is Your "It"? How Do You Find It?

You are more than your life roles, responsibilities, vocation, or financial or educational achievements. You are more than the awards and accolades bestowed on you or any notoriety you have achieved. While significant life events, achievements, and outside acknowledgments have helped shape who you are, below the surface of those milestones there is more. The awareness and appreciation of the individual qualities you used to achieve your accomplishments, your outlook on life, how you express yourself, and what you wish to contribute to the world are what matter most. How do you show the world who you are? Through music, dance, drama, art, the spoken or written word, hobbies, crafting, pottery, cooking, baking, gardening? Self-expression requires you to reach inward, reflect, and pay attention to who you are.

What makes you light up? What speaks to you? What tugs at your heart? It's important to channel your abilities into a form of self-expression that nurtures you. What you bring to the world and how you express it differentiates you from everyone else; nobody can duplicate or express themselves in the same way. Although there are endless possibilities to choose from, it's important to find your "it"—a mode of self-expression that fills you up in inexplicable ways.

What Is Your "It"?

Think of your "it" as a vehicle by which you find a way into you. Your "it" is anything that makes a direct connection to your heart and soul. Your "it" challenges and restores the essence of who you are and captivates you to the point where you can tune out everyone and everything. You may find yourself losing track of time, ignoring hunger, and forgoing sleep. In this instance, not allowing hunger, sleep, or the outside world to distract you is a good thing. The captivation and ability to focus 100 percent is an indication that you have connected with your "it." Engaging in your "it" is a tune-up for your well-being; you are a stronger, wiser, and more efficient person because you engage in your "it." Your "it" ignites the joy within. You can have many "its," and you may discover that even the smallest "it" can yield a big return.

Your "it" doesn't necessarily produce tangible results. For example, one of your "its" might be having organized closets in your home. The anticipated thrill of opening a closet door and the satisfaction you feel gazing at an organized layout is pleasing to you. Or self-care activities, a walk or run, mani-pedi, or wellness retreat might be your "it." As you get closer to your scheduled time of your activity and stay in the present moment, you will feel your joy rising. The objective is to identify what empowers, uplifts, and recharges you. Being mindful of what you are feeling— the anticipation, the experience, and the restorative benefit—is the key to realizing your "it."

Your "its" help to open the door to your authenticity. Authenticity is being clear about who you are;

recognizing your talents, abilities and limitations; knowing what you stand for; and being intentional with how you navigate the world. When who you are aligns with the person you want to be, you have found your authentic self. The connection to our authentic self depends on our ability to look within, self-reflect, and determine what truly matters. Although the connection to your authentic self might take time, it's a connection that offers the gift of personal fulfillment, clarity, and direction in our everyday lives.

Sometimes our authentic self can be easily overlooked or stifled when we listen to everyone else instead of our own voice. Sometimes someone else's dream can get in the way of our own or life throws us curve balls that cause us to lose our way. If you feel that you have not yet found your authentic self, alone time is a must. Dwell in quiet and solitude as outlined in Chapter 4. Get lost in your "its" and remain open. As you nurture and cultivate a relationship with your self, the answers to your authenticity and your "its" will surface.

How to Find Your "Its"

Let's begin your journey to discovering your "it" by awakening those creative pathways inside your brain. Pretend you are housebound and alone for the next couple of days. You've completed your daily tasks and chores, and your cell phone, computer, and TV are turned off. What would you do with this unexpected gift of time? Work on a forgotten project? Write, journal, read? Engross yourself in your hobby? Play an instrument? Draw, paint, or create? Craft, make, or bake? Whatever you choose to do presents another self-discovery clue to the inner you.

If you don't have a clue about what you would do with this time, let's take a trip down memory lane. Think back to your youngest days and revisit your childhood memories and experiences:

- What made you happy?
- What did you love to do endlessly?
- What made you lose track of time?
- What subjects, clubs, projects, and extracurricular activities did you enjoy most in school or outside of school?

Continue contemplating these questions up to the present. Hopefully, this will spark the awareness of activities, accomplishments, and experiences that have brought you fulfillment. Your objective here is to gather clues as to what brings you joy.

Next, let's compose a list of things you love. If Oprah can have her favorite things, so can you! Think about your favorite food, color, season, aroma, flower, gift, activity, setting, outfit, holiday, song, poem, movie, book, style, outing, or place. And please don't discount the littlest things either. For example, I happen to love pajama days, especially during the winter months. You know those days when you stay in your pajamas all day because there is no place you have to be. That is priceless for me. Although this might not resonate with you, I just want to make the point that your list needn't include grandiose things and events. Include the tiniest things that you love too. Over time, as more favorite things pop into your head, keep adding them to your list. This list will set you on your way to your awareness of what matters to you, what you care about, and what is pleasing to your soul.

Keeping the list of your favorite things in mind, let's ponder some additional questions that might get you closer to identifying your "it."

- What do you like to do when you have free time?
- Is there anything you are instantly drawn to or fascinated with?
- What are you passionate about?
- What are your hobbies?
- What activities energize you?
- What do you like to read?
- Do you dream of pursuing another profession?
- What classes would you take for fun?
- What would you regret having never done?
- What three adjectives would you use to describe yourself?

You can download the above questions, "Discovering Your 'Its,'" at https://joselynsmithgreene.com/book-downloads.

Your answers to this inner assessment and your "favorite things" list should offer insight into one or more of your "its." It's a good idea to jot down your thoughts, let some time lapse, revisit them, and add any additional thoughts and ideas you might have.

> At least three times every day take a moment and ask yourself what is really important. Have the wisdom and the courage to build your life around your answer.

—Lee Jampolsky, Author and Psychologist

Discovering My Own "Its"

I have many "its," and thought it would be helpful to share them with you. Writing is at the top of my list. I love to write. I write like a musician plays an instrument, with intent, purpose, feeling, and emotion. Who knew my instrument would be a keyboard—a computer keyboard? Writing is effortless; each letter is a note, and each word is a chord. With each keystroke, I'm one step closer to crafting a melody that exudes my point of view. It gives me pure joy to express who I am from the inside out.

I love to play with words, mixing and matching, arranging and rearranging words and sentences to convey my thoughts in profound ways. Crafting with words requires intention, careful thought, and constant editing. Mostly, I write from my heart, drawing on my personal experiences, both good and bad. Writing can effect change in the most magnificent ways. Perhaps someone will connect with my message, and it will offer them comfort, understanding, or the ability to alter the trajectory of their life. But if the words I write never connect with anyone, that's OK because I had the opportunity to express who I am and seek greater clarity from within.

I didn't always enjoy writing. Throughout high school and college, writing assignments were an inevitable, painful chore. I would focus on the page requirements and panic. I lacked the basic skillset and because I wasn't good at it, the process was always overwhelming. Two things helped changed that: journaling and corresponding with customers. Journaling was a requirement for a high school English class. I began to express myself in the most freeing way, without criticism. Sentence structure, incomplete thoughts, punctuation, and misspelled words didn't matter. The only thing that mattered was that I consistently showed up. After graduating from college, I worked as a consumer correspondent for a sewing pattern company in their customer service department. Writing detailed, descriptive content in a concise, systematic format was a major part of my job. These two divergent writing experiences honed my writing abilities. Over time, the ability to express myself became easier and easier. The more I expressed myself, the more I got to know myself. Journaling and writing encourages me to look within, self-reflect, and be mindful. It is the reason I write and journal today.

Another one of my "its" is making things. I have a deep appreciation for all things handmade. The design, planning, and manifestation of an idea from conception to production captivates me. Engaging in the creative process with no limits or boundaries and experimenting with materials literally make my heart swell. The unexpected results and unintended destinations encountered through creative play are great preparation for the stumbling blocks, uncertainty, and imperfect moments found in the everyday.

One of my favorite experiences was time spent at my local neighborhood community center. The arts and crafts room was my haven, where I dabbled in a little of everything. It had a huge walk-in supply closet filled with paints, crayons, a variety of papers, lanyards, Popsicle sticks, craft kits, and so much more. To this day, I can remember spinning around in that closet in awe of all the creative materials I had to choose from. I can even remember the smell. It was better than being a kid in a candy store. After making a selection, I would sit at a huge butcher block work table and create. It was a magical time and place to be, where I could be worry-free.

I started sewing at the age of 10. When I was 12, my sister went away for the summer. To make up for her absence, I constructed a life-size doll from fabric remnants and yarn to keep me company. At 13, I made outfits that I wore to school. By high school, I made most of my clothing, including coats and jackets. But one of my best maker experiences was when I interviewed for the job with the pattern company I mentioned previously. I had been using their patterns for many years. My brand-new college degree wasn't as important as my ability to sew and my familiarity with their product. I had the bright idea of wearing a suit I made using one of their patterns to the interview. When asked about my knowledge of their product, I referred to my suit. Eyebrow raised, the interviewer was impressed and offered me the job.

Sewing helped elevate my self-esteem at a time when I was at my lowest. When I wasn't excelling in school, my ability to take fabric and notions to create a one-of-a-kind outfit made me feel talented and accomplished. When I was in my zone, the only thing I was thinking about was the garment that was materializing step by step. Sewing initiated the start of my superpower persona. The admiration from others was the pat on the back that allowed me to hang on. The opportunity to create was where I found my joy.

> All around you are ordinary moments and experiences that could be extraordinary just by your love and attention.

—Barbara Brown Taylor, Author, Professor, and Priest

My early crafting experiences and learning to sew at a young age are why I experiment creatively today. Is it any wonder that my most-loved childhood gifts were a stencil/paint set, sewing machine, and knitting machine? Today, nostalgia sets in when I enter a hardware, fabric, or craft store and peruse the aisles of raw materials and creative supplies. Immediately, I go to a happy place as my mind floods with ideas and possibilities.

Although sewing is my first love, it opened the door to experimenting with other maker activities: crochet, embroidery, upholstery, furniture refinishing. Years later, I became drawn to the do-it-yourself arena. Today, I love to create, re-create, and repurpose. It's a part of who I am. I am not an expert in any one area. Perfection is not my intent. Instead, I have learned to embrace perfect imperfection. The experience of stripping the layers from a piece of furniture, while simultaneously peeling back the layers of my being, is the intent. As I work with my hands, I'm working on myself, reflecting, praying, meditating, feeling, and growing. Creating offers me a place of joyous, mental solace; a feeling like no other that fills me up and restores my soul.

Another Approach to Finding Your "It"

If you are still having trouble pinpointing your "it," let's try another approach. Questioning ourselves without restrictions frees our mind to wander through unchartered territories without limits. So, for the next set of questions, pretend you are not bound by financial restraints and have zero responsibilities and nobody to answer to. Just resist the urge to include shopping sprees, spa visits, or living the life of the rich and famous in your answers. Taking this approach, how would you respond to the following questions?

- How would you spend the hours of each day?
- Would you stay in your current profession?
- Would you go back to school?
- Would you champion a philanthropic or charitable cause?
- Would you effect change in the world?
- Would you start a business?
- Would you walk away from a business?

But don't just ask the easy questions. It is the difficult ones that will allow you to dig below the surface to connect with your inner self and reveal what's important to you. Here are a few to consider:

- Can you think of a time when someone or something discouraged you from doing something you wanted to do?
- Was there a time when you felt like you were on top of the world but circumstances overshadowed your joy?
- Do you regret giving up on a goal or dream that you felt could have been life-changing?
- Do you entertain "what if" scenarios in your head? If so, about what?

Questions like these will allow you to reflect on your story and help you to reach inside to discover clues that point to your "its."

Be patient with yourself during this process. Be mindful and use the alone time we discussed in Chapter 4 to journal about your answers. Freeing yourself to entertain thoughts that may be a stretch beyond your everyday is necessary to discover your "its."

You can download the above prompts, "Questions Without Restrictions," at https://joselynsmithgreene.com/book-downloads.

Still Stuck?

Now that you have begun the process of developing a connection from within, you have likely gained additional insight or have a better understanding of who you are. On the other hand, if you find yourself stuck or your answers are not exactly on point, consider opening yourself to new experiences. Dabble in things outside of your norm, being mindful of what instantly engages you until you find your "it" or a mode of self-expression that aligns with your authentic self.

You might find that you love various methods of self-expression. You might start out with one mode and, over time, find other modes to add to your repertoire. What's most important is to leave yourself open to all possibilities that allow you to express yourself. Look at it as a journey within your life's journey. You have no idea where each path is going to take you or what you may learn. Your results, projects, compositions, or efforts might not necessarily develop into what you intended or score a home run in your eyes, but an unexpected or lackluster outcome doesn't matter. It's not about hitting the ball out of the park. It's about you and how the process molded, changed, and impacted the essence of who you are. Think of indulging in your favorite activity as a tune-up for your internal maintenance. But remember that your "it" doesn't have to appeal to anyone else, just you. Does this mode of self-expression enhance your life's story? Does it evoke fond memories or link to one or more of your defining moments? If your "it" serves you, and by that I mean it elevates and fills you up till your cup runneth over, then you've found what makes you, you.

Using my creative prowess to problem solve, and compensate for my weaknesses is a part of who I am. It's one of my "its." To illustrate my point, I will revisit my graduate school experience mentioned in Chapter 3. Although I had been out of college for 8 years and I was working full time, my desire to go to graduate school never waned. That desire motivated me to pursue a job at New York University. After being offered a position, I knew I was one step closer to realizing my graduate degree. But I also knew getting accepted was going to be a hurdle, given my track record with standardized tests. Years earlier, I had taken the GMAT, and it came as no surprise that my score was dismal. Determined to find a way, I continued to research all opportunities NYU had to offer. I found a program that didn't require a GRE or GMAT score for entry. I applied and was accepted. It was the beginning of another defining moment. My creative resourcefulness fueled my ability to pursue my dream in a different way.

Don't Let Constraints Stop You

As mentioned earlier, I didn't allow my standardized test scores to stop me from attending graduate school. By thinking outside the box, I kept the door open to possibility and danced around my constraints. Hopefully, you will be able to pursue your "it" within the confines of your current lifestyle and everyday responsibilities. But don't dismiss your "it" if it isn't attainable within your present circumstances. If your "it" exceeds any personal, financial, or time restrictions you might have, it's time to put your thinking cap on and explore ways to experience your "it" in a way that's conducive to your lifestyle. For example, say you love nature, but you live in a city with very little greenery. Maybe there is a botanical garden or green space that you can visit regularly or volunteer at. You enjoy gourmet food, but your budget doesn't allow for dining out. How about mastering those gourmet dishes at home and inviting friends for a night in instead? We are all familiar with the proverb that necessity is the mother of invention, but I challenge you to allow constraints to be the daughter of creativity. Be open to alternative approaches to living your "it." Be still, dream, and allow yourself to find a way.

Constraints are an opportunity to grow. When my husband and I, with baby number 2 on the way, bought our home, the down payment and closing expenses exhausted our savings. The furniture we had didn't work well in the new space and new home furnishings were out of the question. Thankfully, the do-it-yourself movement was gaining popularity and thrift store and flea market shopping became in vogue. This ignited my flame and fueled my interest and passion for trash-to-treasure redesign. I began refinishing, upcycling, and upholstering furniture. It was empowering and cathartic. Whenever I am in the garage working on a project, I get lost in the doing. My "to-do" list goes away. My mind becomes clear and open for reflection. The art of trash-to-treasure goes way beyond upcycling, restoring, or making something pretty; the process was and still is a demonstration of physical and personal creativity, redemption, and reinvention. Furnishing a home on a budget not only turned into an enjoyable, rewarding, and fulfilling way to express myself, but it also offered an inner contentment as well.

The Why Behind My "Its"

Equally important to discovering your "it" is the why behind your "it." Why is your "it" your "it"? My love for creativity originated from the need to escape the negative messages I received as a child. My love for writing, which began with journaling, gave me my voice when nobody bothered to listen. Both these passions, my "its," helped me revamp my personal narrative to understand who I am and be clear about who I choose to be. Contemplating "why" fosters a greater connection to who you are. Why does your "it" drive you? Why does your "it" speak to you and grab your attention? How and why does your "it" serve you? We are drawn to things for a reason. That reason is at the root of our why and may be due to previous life experiences or present circumstances. That reason is where your authenticity lies.

As you gain clarity into who you are, your "its," and the why behind your "its," the next step is weaving your "its" into your life. The more you can incorporate your "its" into your everyday life, the more aligned you will be with living authentically.

EXERCISE 5

WHAT'S YOUR WHY?

Again, let's consider your backstory. Review your responses to Exercise 3 in Chapter 3 and ask yourself whether your experiences:

- allowed you to demonstrate your ability to persevere?
- offered you peace and solitude?
- gave you an opportunity to exercise your creativity?
- initiated the start of a personal evolution or served as evidence of internal growth?
- inspired you?
- motivated you?
- affirmed who you are?

The above questions will help you extrapolate the "why" and the underlying factors that reside beneath the surface of our backstory. There are always stories behind our choices and what we gravitate toward. Reflecting on our backstory can be helpful to understanding ourselves, what we truly love, and what sustains us.

WHAT IS YOUR "IT"? HOW DO YOU FIND IT?

❝

Who looks outside, dreams; who looks inside, awakes.

—Carl Jung

> Everything that happens in the universe starts with intention.

—Deepak Chopra

CHAPTER 6

How Do You Want to Show Up to the World?

The self-discovery exercises and questions provided throughout this book are designed to offer you an understanding and appreciation for your individual authenticity. Hopefully your journaling and alone time have given you an opportunity to look inward and connect with your authenticity as well. Your ability to achieve clarity about who you are and what matters enables you to share your special greatness with the world.

Curating Your Vision

Creating a vision board is an excellent way to solidify your self-discovery findings. A vision board is a graphic representation of you: your truths, dreams, goals, aspirations, and your "its." It can easily be made using a poster or cork board or, if you prefer, you can design a digital board. Creating both "old school" and digital versions gives you the ability to display your vision board in your personal dedicated space (as outlined in Chapter 4), as well as on your electronic devices for daily viewing. A carefully curated vision board reinforces your ability to be intentional with your attention and to weed out the things that don't align with who you are. You remain focused on who you are, your "it," and what truly matters.

Curating a vision board is a fun part of your self-discovery process and a chance to tap into your inner creativity. You have full editorial control—no judgments, rules, time restrictions, grades, or criticism. But even though you have full rein, be aware of the possibility of personal sabotage. We can be our own worst critic, so I encourage you to be fully present and make a conscious effort to silence any negativity. If the thought "I'm not creative" pops into your head or graces your lips, please don't listen. Instead, turn it around and affirm, "I am creative." Don't let self-limiting thoughts prevent you from connecting with the real you. Negativity won't serve you. It will only hold you back. What will serve you is an authentic visual representation of who you are.

As many of us probably learned to cut and paste during our earliest years, this is the perfect opportunity to channel that inner child. Pretend you're in elementary school, with no inhibitions and a blank board placed before you. How do you wish to fill it? Start with things you love, layer it with things that matter to you, and see what develops and unfolds. Use magazines, drawings, quotes, mantras, text, images, and whatever else you can think of to create your personalized visual. As you fill the board, do you notice any patterns or clues emerging? Don't overthink; instead be carefree. Change your mind about something or find something that matters more? Edit, edit, edit. Never stop editing because your personal vision and journey is a continuous progression and where your greatness resides.

Recognizing the Greatness Within You

Greatness isn't just about the big and the wow; it's also about the small and the now. Putting grandiosity aside, consider the little things you love doing that allow you to connect with the inner you and others. For example, maybe you enjoy planning intimate gatherings at your home. Or you have a talent or an expertise that could be used by your community or an organization whose mission aligns with what matters to you. Or perhaps you have a desire to meet with people who share a common interest or goal. Your authenticity and greatness reside in the little nuances within you that not only elevate you but can also inspire others. Using and sharing what you enjoy to serve and benefit others is a manifestation of your greatness.

If you're not feeling your greatness just yet, maybe the following questions will get you started:

- How would you describe yourself?
- When you are in the presence of family, friends, or even strangers, what do people notice about you?
- Like the sweet smell of a cake baking in the oven or a whiff of your favorite scent wafting through the air, what presence do you command?
- What is your personal aesthetic? (Describe how you see yourself and how you want others to see you.)
- What are your life's intentions?

You can download the above questions, "Recognizing Your Greatness," at https://joselynsmithgreene.com/book-downloads.

> It is no bad thing celebrating a simple life.

—J.R.R. Tolkien

Be You, Love You, Brand You

Once you begin identifying and tapping into your unique qualities, let's take it a step further and discuss personal branding. Just as companies create brands to evoke a thought, feeling, experience, or memory to make a connection between their product or service and their customers, we can do the same for ourselves to better understand and project who we are.

Not sure how to begin the personal branding process? Here's an idea I came up with during one of my still and quiet moments, and it's a perfect segue from your vision board: a *YOU*r Story Kit. Like a publicity kit that presents a company's overall image, message, and focus, a *YOU*r Story Kit captures and showcases the essence of who you are, showcasing your unique qualities in a fun and innovative way. It's up to you what you want to include in *YOU*r Story Kit, but here are a few suggestions. (You can see the kit I designed for myself at the end of the chapter.)

- *YOU*r Story Card: Like a business card, this is a short summary of who *you* are. Company information and job title are replaced with abbreviated responses to "Who are you?," "What is your 'it'?," and "Why is your 'it' your 'it'?" (as discussed in Chapter 5). Since you are confined to a small surface area, your content needs to be concise and carefully curated to a few powerful words or short phrases.
- *YOU*r Personal Statement: A statement or pitch that summarizes who you are what you're about,

and what is important to you, without using the usual labels and categories referenced in Chapter 2. It doesn't have to be long; a paragraph is more than enough.

- ***YOU*r Mission Statement:** This is your reason for being on this planet. It's an account of what you want to accomplish or have in store for your life going forward.
- ***YOU*r Logo/Crest:** This is a visual symbol of your life's purpose, evolution, journey, and legacy. Drawing skills are not required. You can use clip art or images and text from magazines.
- ***YOU*r Personal Anthem:** This is a song or poem that connects to the inner you and aligns with who you are and your mission statement. If the lyrics or words tug at your heart, stir you up, and propel you into a feel-good state no matter what is going on in your life, that is your anthem. Choose songs or poems that immediately bring you to the present moment and whose lyrics affirm "I got you" and reinforce "yes you can." Curate a "Personal Anthem" playlist that will elevate your state of mind and pick you up during tough times.

The content among the items in *YOU*r Story Kit will likely overlap. The most important thing is to be creative with your approach and, above all, have fun! By the way, if you have trouble starting or are scrambling for ideas, just Google your way through any roadblocks you encounter. Allow your ideas to surface. If you find it easier to begin the process using a traditional business format, it's a start.

HOW DO YOU WANT TO SHOW UP TO THE WORLD?

> Why is it great to create?
> - It's enjoyable.
> - It opens new ideas.
> - It exercises our brain.
> - It makes us happy.

— Jon Burgerman, NYC Doodling Artist and Author

You can always personalize it later to reflect your message, personal story, and vision. The most important thing is to keep questioning yourself about what you stand for, what you want to project, and the way you want to share your unique and special point of view with the world.

If you remember, I began Chapter 2 asking the question "who are you?" in the absence of family or job title, marital status, life responsibilities, gender, ethnicity, religious affiliation, or any other common descriptor. Sure, I am a wife, mother, operations manager, etc., but who I am—my authentic self—exceeds those roles.

My kit focuses on the following personal statements and the qualities and beliefs I identify with:

- Creative visionary, observer, idea generator
- Drawn to individuality and uniqueness
- Writer, quote lover, and champion for self-expression
- Lover of all books, especially those with blank pages to fill
- DIY-obsessed, handmade enthusiast, graphics connoisseur
- Jane of all trades, master of some
- Believer in the power of love, redemption, and transformation

Just as it's necessary to revise a resume, the elements of YOUr Story Kit may require tweaks to reflect the evolution of your authentic self, personal discoveries, and journey. To avoid losing sight of "you," keep YOUr Story Kit in your daily view along with your vision board.

HOW DO YOU WANT TO SHOW UP TO THE WORLD?

YOUr
STORY CARD

Joselyn with an "**s**"

Creative Junkie

Quote Collector

Writer & **J**ournaler

Personal **S**tory **A**dvocate

THE GIFT OF KNOWING YOU

YOUR PERSONAL ANTHEM

My faves..............

Poetry

The Road Not Taken
Robert Frost

Rise Up
Andra Day

Songs

The Voice Within
Christine Aguilera

Still I Rise
Maya Angelou

Stand
Bebe Winans

I Dwell in Possibility
Emily Dickinson

quotes ♥ inspire

HOW DO YOU WANT TO SHOW UP TO THE WORLD?

YOUR MISSION STATEMENT

Mission............

I live to **Inspire** others

to **Journey** within,

Connect with their story,

Value who they are and

Realize their **Joy.**

THE GIFT OF KNOWING YOU

YOUr
LOGO/CREST

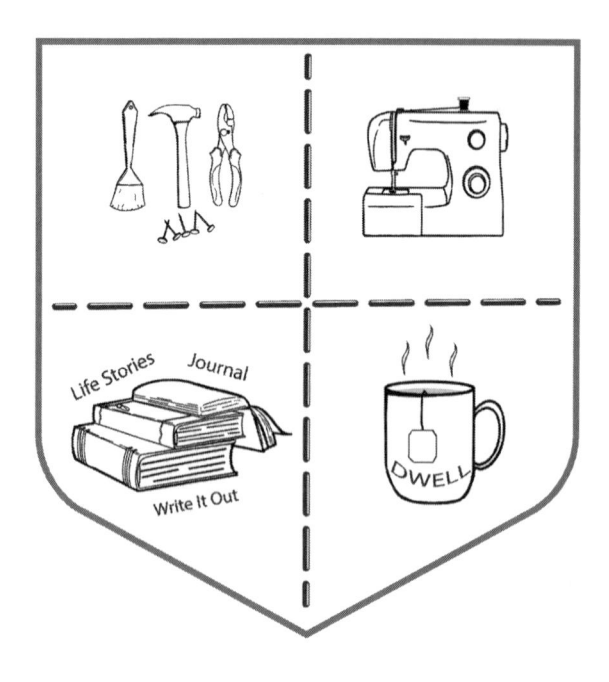

HOW DO YOU WANT TO SHOW UP TO THE WORLD?

YOUr
PERSONAL STATEMENT

Who I am

— — — — — — — — — — — — —

Creative Visionary, observer, idea generator
Drawn to individuality and uniqueness

Writer, quote lover, and champion for
self-expression

Lover of all books, especially those with blank
pages to fill

DIY obsessed, handmade enthusiast, graphics
connoisseur

Jane of all trades, master of some

Believer in the power of love, redemption, and
transformation

— — — — — — — — — — — — —

beyond my everyday roles and responsibilities

> We must accommodate changing times but cling to principles that never change.

—Jimmy Carter, quoting his high school teacher

CHAPTER 7

How Do You Continue the Journey?

Relevance can be a game changer. It is the antithesis of stagnation, requiring us to evolve through societal and generational changes, embrace the unknown, and step into uncharted territory. Our ability to stay relevant closes the divide between ourselves and the rest of the world, helping us to stay anchored in the present and in the best position to offer the world our greatest contributions at each stage of our lives.

I'm not suggesting that any of us abandon our personal truths or condone everything the present has to offer. Our coming-of-age experiences will always be remembered in the best light, while each new generation will seemingly appear to have lost their way, fueling the generational divide. Older and younger generations are convinced neither has a clue. When we discount what each generation has to offer, we are shortchanging ourselves and society. Think about this: Older people have a solid body of life experiences and know more about the things that don't change, while younger people know more about the things that are constantly changing. Everyone has something valuable to offer.

> The purpose of life is to discover your gift. The work of life is to develop it. The meaning of life is to give your gift away.

—David S. Viscot, Media Personality, Author and Psychiatrist

Think about personal relevance as the contribution you make to lessening the generational divide. By remaining individually relatable to the present, we avoid wallowing in observer mode, retaining our ability to contribute and make a difference, thriving instead of merely existing. Our abilities will morph and change throughout our lifetime but making a conscious effort to stay connected within the confines of our abilities allows us to remain fully engaged in our everyday lives.

Relevance and connection reside in the doing—establishing and making personal connections, taking action that aligns with our personal truths, and giving others the opportunity to benefit from our life story. The art of doing fosters creativity and openness to finding ways to stay in the moment, being conscious of our perceptions, listening to our inner voice of our best self, and sharing our thought processes. We can empower ourselves to use our mental currency, the sum of our life experiences packaged with our gifts, talents, and "its," to become a welcomed blessing to others.

Befriending all generations allows us to fully understand the changing world in which we live, as well as the ability to actively participate in our everyday lives. We can do this by extending one hand to the generations that precede us and the other hand to the generations that follow. An authentic connection to others depends on our ability to understand the human condition of all ages, at any age.

Surrounding ourselves with people who don't look like the reflection we see in the mirror and immersing ourselves in different points of view help us cultivate a societal foundation that intertwines racial, cultural, and generational lines. One of the best gifts we can give ourselves and the world is to participate in the erosion of the divide between ourselves and those who are different from us. Each of us has a significant and unique story that's worthy of being acknowledged, shared, and understood. Healthy human interaction is not making the world more like us but helping others to be the best of who they are and appreciating them as they are without judgment. Understandably, sometimes this can be difficult, giving way to internal strife and struggle. Being mindful, present, and honest about our thoughts and feelings is what's most important. We can learn so much from each other if we keep our hearts and the human doors of exchange open.

The Journey Continues

Life is a journey full of planned and unplanned destinations. Writing this book is part of my journey, just as reading this book is part of your journey. If we remain open, our being is in constant transformation—learning, growing, and evolving into what we were put on this earth to become, our authentic selves. At any given time, the journey can be exciting, scary, happy, sad, or one big unnerving question mark! Our receptiveness and our connection to self directly influence the paths we choose along the way. Life is a continuum of events, shaping who we are, full of opportunities to reach our highest self and identify our true calling.

> Transformation is a process, and as life happens, there are tons of ups and downs. It's a journey of discovery. There are moments on mountaintops and moments in deep valleys of despair.

—Rick Warren, Pastor

Whether we jump over the hurdles or are deterred by obstacles is our choosing. When presented with a bumpy ride, we can choose to hold on and ride it out as best we can or fight the inevitable, realizing that what we resist will only persist. Or we can choose to embrace a "this too shall pass" mindset, knowing that the light at the end of the tunnel will reveal itself if we are patient, choose faith, and keep our hearts and minds open. Over time, things will shift and lessons will be learned, giving us a greater ability to create the change we need and desire. If we grow and morph into exactly who we were destined to become, we are in our best position to craft the life we want for ourselves.

When our journey hits a sweet patch and we are mindful, we can appreciate each present moment and savor it like a sweet, dark cherry because our next destination might not be as sweet. Life is so full of itsy-bitsy pieces of goodness—an inspiring conversation, an unscheduled moment to just be, a smile, a thank you—that are easily overlooked due to the busyness of our days. By choosing mindfulness and valuing these small gifts of joy, they can have a more profound effect than all the big "wows" in our lives. We must remind ourselves to be present and participate in each moment with our eyes and hearts wide open.

It's important to make a conscious effort to stay connected with ourselves. Our intuition warrants our full attention and allows us to distinguish between what is and what is not in our best interest. By choosing to listen to our internal cheerleading dialogue, along with hard work, determination, and perseverance, we can accomplish anything we set our minds to. We can also recognize the ugly naysayer dialogue and eradicate the destructive content without internalizing the negativity.

What's Your Legacy?

Our time on this earth is limited. Establishing a legacy holds us accountable to our authentic self. We can use our talents, gifts, and experiences to give back and make the world a better place. If you have never given any thought to your legacy, perhaps the following questions will get you started:

- What do you want the world to remember most about you?
- What gifts do you want to leave behind so others can have a better life because of the life you lived?
- What do you want to accomplish in your life?
- What matters to you?
- What would you like to change?
- What character values are most important to you?

Answers to these questions will begin to reveal the foundation for your legacy. If you nurture the relationship with your authentic self, your legacy—your gift to the world—will benefit others.

You can download the above questions, "What's Your Legacy?," at https://joselynsmithgreene.com/book-downloads.

> You have no idea what your legacy will be. Your legacy is every life that has been uplifted, been moved, or not been moved by everything you did.

—Maya Angelou

The Connection Within

I want to encourage others to create the life they envisioned for themselves, and I hope this book will help jumpstart the process. Struggles, pain, and obstacles are part of life, but with perseverance and faith, triumph can prevail. Happiness need not be predicated on a bank account, material possessions, or a fancy job title. How we feel about ourselves, our outlook on life, and whether our lives are in sync with our authenticity are of greater importance.

When we connect with our internal dialog, we learn the truth about who we are, how we see ourselves, and the "whys" behind our daily interactions. There is a reason something or somebody triggers a pleasant or unpleasant response, or why we shy away from tough questions, or dismiss our uncensored raw responses. Reflecting on our interactions and reactions offers clues about who we are. Why did I react in that manner? Why am I uncomfortable? Why am I sad? Why am I nervous? Why didn't I stand up for myself? Why does this make me happy? Why am I feeling this way? Openness, honesty, and mindfulness are key to realizing our self-discovery revelations.

Since the eyes are the windows to our soul, before starting your day, look in the mirror. Make eye contact with your reflection. Stare intently for a minute or two. Are you content with what you see? Not from a physical standpoint, but from one of self-love. As you look in the mirror, be aware of your internal dialogue. What do you say to you about you? Is it easy to recite positive affirmations to your reflection? "I am smart. I am kind. I am beautiful." I am capable. I am well. I am thankful. I am worthy. I am confident. I am talented. I am enough. I matter." Do you feel the words you speak? Really feel them? Or do you find it difficult to shower yourself with self-loving affirmations? If it presents a problem, there's an easy fix: Practice, practice, practice. Say it and write it until you believe it. Love and accept yourself as you are. Believe that you are worthy of your time and affirmative words. Engage in a self-discovery process that offers you the gift of knowing you.

My ease into self-discovery came from journaling and creating. I can still remember my first journal, given to me when I was very young. It had a brown leather cover and gold-rimmed pages with a miniature lock and key. And then there was the high school journaling practice I mentioned earlier. It took place in a marble composition notebook. All these years later, I can only imagine the horror on my teacher's face when she read my entries. I was brutally honest, and it didn't occur to me to be a little more selective about what I wrote. In hindsight, though, I'm glad I didn't edit myself. My journal became a place where I could vent and let it all out. It was the release I needed. I was a sad, angry, and resentful teenager who had a war raging inside. It was ugly, but journaling got me through. It kept me from indulging in drugs, alcohol, etc. for solace.

> Journal writing gives us insights into who we are, who we were, and who we can become.

—Sandra Marinella, Author

Thankfully, my journal was returned to me without judgment or criticism. It wasn't until much later that I realized how important that journaling experience and practice contributed to my ability to express my thoughts, transform my anger, and find peace within. I still prefer to journal in a composition notebook. It continues to serve as a place where I can let go, connect, and be true to myself.

Today I'm in a good place, I love who I am, and I am truly grateful for life's tiniest moments. It's important to find and process one's truth. Had I not released those negative feelings and emotions through journaling, I would still be wallowing in all that old stuff, carrying around excess baggage and holding myself back from who I was meant to be. If I hadn't faced the truth, I wouldn't have experienced the breakthroughs and exercised the forgiveness necessary to live my best life.

Why Not Give It a Try?

If you encounter any trouble connecting with the inner you, I highly recommend journaling. It's a perfect way to stimulate healthy internal dialogue and seek clarity. When researching the benefits of journaling, I discovered a myriad of references to studies and abstracts indicating the benefits of expressive writing, particularly regarding health: for example, lower blood pressure, a strengthened immune system, and stress reduction. But rather than relying on clinical research or even my positive journaling experience, what would it hurt to give it a try?

HOW DO YOU CONTINUE THE JOURNEY?

> Whatever follows, 'I am' will eventually find you.

—Joel Osteen, Pastor

Documenting the biographical events of your day in a chronological format is the most common type of journaling, but there are other types as well, each offering a unique benefit:

- **Stream-of-consciousness journaling** is a good release for all the excess, unimportant thoughts that detract from your present-moment thoughts. It's a brain dump where you write down your uncensored thoughts without scrutinizing, thinking, or editing them. It's not supposed to make sense and will most likely sound and look like gibberish. Stream-of-consciousness journaling rids you of the useless stuff knocking around in your head that interferes with your ability to be mindful and fully present.
- **Affirmational journaling** is a feel-good, empowering practice that helps counteract the internal negative dialogue and the limiting beliefs we might be clinging to. The focus becomes the positive qualities you wish to reinforce. I am enough, I am talented, I am loved, I am worthy. Whatever you are struggling with, whatever limiting belief you have been telling yourself, affirmational journaling is a way to transform a negative personal narrative into a positive one.
- **Gratitude journaling** is simple, exponentially life-changing, and ups your mindfulness factor. Although this practice may initially begin with acknowledging the big stuff, like a vacation, a lavish present, or a major purchase, with practice and consistency, it will quickly trickle down to small things,

like the warmth of the sun, a blooming flower, the deliciousness of a favorite treat, or a few minutes of unexpected alone time. What's so wonderful about this practice is that gratitude begets more gratitude. The more you practice gratitude, the more grateful you become.
- **Self-reflection journaling** is more thought-intensive. The intent is to connect and assess what you're feeling and experiencing at any given time within your life story. From the smallest moments to the life-changing experiences, each one matters because it contributed to the person you are today. Self-reflection journaling is a freeing emotional release offering the space to sort and work through your feelings, and in so doing, strengthen the connection to self.
- **Commonplace journaling** is a collection of your thoughts, ideas, observations, memories, dreams, aspirations, goals, responses, doodles, etc. If something (i.e., a quote or passage) or someone grabs your attention and makes you ponder, journal about it. You can include scrapbook-worthy ephemera from your life too. As you fill the pages of your commonplace journal, a visual of your individuality will unfold.

If you are unsure about where to begin the journaling process, revisit some of the defining moments in your life: those moments, good or bad, that changed your trajectory. Look through any photos, scrapbooks, and memorabilia you might have. As memories begin to resurface, write about them. Start with the easiest questions—who, what, where, when, and why—then think about those same experiences on a deeper level:

- How did it make you feel?
- How did it change your outlook on life?
- Did it make you a stronger person?
- Was it empowering?
- Did it detract from who you are?
- Did it make you feel better/worse about yourself?

Don't be tempted to acknowledge only the great experiences; it's necessary to acknowledge the not-so-great ones as well. When you revisit your feelings, particularly unresolved hurtful ones, it's going to sting. How could it not? You're reliving something you might have tucked away or suppressed to cope or get on with your life. Unraveling and reliving those feelings might be painful, but allowing the distress to fester inside you is destructive to your soul. If you find yourself struggling with the process or your feelings, toughing it out is not the answer. Talk, consult, and open yourself to the personal and professional assistance of others. The key is to be mindful. It's going to take time and perhaps some of your cheerleaders to see you through past hurts. Journaling is an opportunity to look within, discard the junk and negativity, listen to your heart, and maintain your inner clarity.

You can download the above questions, "Defining Moments," at https://joselynsmithgreene.com/book-downloads.

> You are the star of your life story.

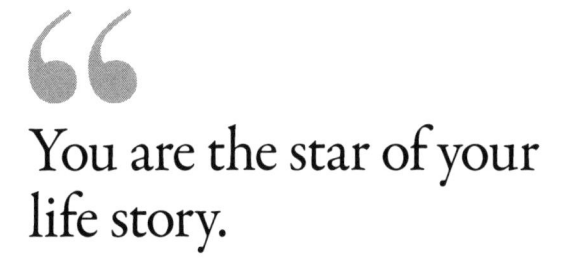

—Joselyn Smith-Greene

Your Star Performance

The internet and social media make it easy for celebrities and other people's lives to occupy our thoughts. If we are not careful, we can unknowingly become more interested in their lives and less interested in our own. There is a fine line between curiosity and obsession, especially if we are not aware of our addiction to wanting to know more. The good news is we can turn this dynamic around and choose to be the celebrities in our own lives. We are capable of great performances if we decide to show up for our audience of one, ourselves, and be our own fan and the sole member of our own academy. We can champion ourselves for our greatness and acknowledge the internal applause within.

Showing up for our personal dramas and the up-close and present-moment live performances, where there is no "Take 2," requires precision and personal commitment. It's not easy deciding whether we will take the starring or supportive role. It's not easy opening ourselves to scrutiny. And it's not easy revealing our true authentic self. If we make the decision to stay present, one moment at a time, we can hone our craft of showcasing our best selves, delivering our best performances each time for ourselves and the world.

With each performance comes a review from our internal voice. Be mindful of which one you are listening to. The internal critic will sabotage us and make us second-guess ourselves, if we allow it. The cheerleader voice is always kind, loving, and patient. We can decide for ourselves if we are worthy of true EGOT status that has nothing to do with an Emmy, Grammy, Oscar, or Tony. Rather, we can ask ourselves, are we striving for *Excellence*? *Giving* to ourselves and others? *Open* to life's possibilities and *Thankful* for the tiniest blessings life bestows upon us? Yes to all the above? Take a bow, you deserve it! Success need not be defined by magnanimous things and events. Remember, the small things we do every day matter too. It's not about the big and the wow, it's about the small and the now.

You Are Worthy

Are you open? Feeling worthy? Are you ready to live a life intentionally crafted by you? Everyone deserves that. You deserve that. Affirm every day, "I am worthy, and I matter!" Be mindful of your body's response to these deserving affirmations. Are they welcomed by your soul, or is there resistance? Metaphorically speaking, when you can feel these positive affirmations attaching to your DNA, not only do you become inspired for greatness, but you will want to inspire others as well.

As you dwell in possibility and live a conscious connected life, you clear the way for living your best life. Cultivate your cheerleader voice. Dismiss the negative voices and the external naysayers as neither have a vested interest in your ability to craft your best life. You don't have to prove yourself to anyone, command respect, or seek the approval of outsiders to justify who you are. You are a dynamic work in progress, molding, shaping, and growing as you travel along your journey. Every step you take to nourish who you are strengthens the internal connection you have to your inner self.

There's nobody else exactly like you, and that's rather special. Once you identify and connect with your authentic specialness, feel your worthiness from within, and incorporate it into your every day, you're there. You're well on your way to knowing the real you. Enjoy the magnificent journey to discovering all of who you are.

HOW DO YOU CONTINUE THE JOURNEY?

> Everybody has a story, and there's something to be learned from every experience.

—Oprah Winfrey

> When you forgive, you heal, when you let go, you grow.

—Annonymous

CHAPTER 8

Transforming Darkness into Light

It took a long time to come to terms with the diseased relationship I shared with my father. Thoughts about my earliest years used to make me angry, always bringing tears to my eyes. It was at those moments I opened my journal, confronted the upset, and wrote about what I was feeling. Journaling enabled me to work through my unresolved pain. I journaled away the bad stuff, prayed for better tomorrows, and promised myself that my fractured childhood would be the gateway to a functional adulthood.

Once I was on my own and in control of my life, it was up to me to turn around my broken past. Doing so required making peace with the past by acknowledging the hurt, exercising forgiveness, and letting the pain go. I realized that my father wasn't a bad man. He was a broken man who didn't have the self-awareness or the tools to address his brokenness. Thankfully, I flipped the script and gifted myself in adulthood what I didn't experience in my childhood. I deserved a life where internal peace reigns; self-love, self-care, and self-worth prevails; and intention is at the forefront of my thoughts and actions. I created a life that I look forward to living.

> The primary cause of unhappiness is never the situation but your thoughts about it.

—Eckhart Tolle

Although I didn't know it at the time, faith and prayer also served as my lifeline. Even though I felt trapped in my pain, I would pray moment by moment to endure the difficult and dark moments. Now my moment-to-moment prayers are mostly thank yous. Thank you for seeing me through. Thank you for the ability to lead a conscious life allowing feelings, both good and bad, to surface and be acknowledged. Thank you for a life filled with tiny blessings and welcomed tomorrows.

A belief system is important in the quest to know who we are, how we fit into the world, and who we are destined to be. That belief system includes the stories we tell ourselves, our code of conduct, the way we navigate life, what we rely on when life is unkind, and how we give thanks when life is sweet. A belief system provides a foundation for living consciously, taking ownership of our lives, assessing who we are as human beings, and determining our place in the world.

Allowing ourselves to be still and quiet is crucial to exposing the layers of our lives that might otherwise cause us to hide or cover up our story. If we don't know our truest self, how can we expect others to know and understand who we are? Layer by layer, feeling the hurt and pain we have endured, chapter by chapter of our story, is key. The greatest challenge lies in our ability to prevent the pain from overshadowing the joyous times or deterring the connection to our truest self. As bad as pain and unpleasant experiences make us feel, they can have the greatest and most profound impact on our lives. Whether that impact is positive or negative depends on our willingness to confront and examine every detail, every emotion, and every thought, and use them toward our personal healing and betterment.

When I was that unhappy little girl, I remember entering the neat and tidy homes of friends permeated with laughter, serenity, and love. When I stepped across their thresholds, it was as if I was swept into an internal and external hug simultaneously. I remember how good it felt to be a part of such warm surroundings, however briefly, in awe and wonder. It was inviting, yet foreign. It was not my reality.

Many years later, after removing the rose-colored glasses, I realized that things are not always what they seem. The happy family living in that neat and tidy home was not as happy as I made them out to be. Nobody's story is picture-perfect and pain-free. The stories in my head didn't necessarily match the realities. The perfection I created in my mind was born out of a necessity to dream a life filled with peace, contentment, and promise. It was my survival tactic, my way of seeking refuge from the unhappiness, turmoil, and frustration circulating in and around me.

One of my greatest triumphs has been the ability to transform my not-so-great yesterdays into happy-just-because tomorrows. It took a lot of forgiveness, self-reflection, honesty, and personal exchange to repair my brokenness. It is from my experience that I offer two takeaways. First, be mindful of your backstory. Wherever it falls on the spectrum, good, bad or somewhere in between, you and I are products of our story. Second, pain can be transformative, if we allow it to be.

Questioning, self-reflection, and self-discovery are key to connecting with who we are. Discovering and living with purpose is our ticket to living authentically and inspiring others to do the same. Knowing what matters to us and what we stand for, as well as being aware of life's tiniest moments, is the foundation on which we can create our best lives.

*Realize the gifts within you;
you were put on this Earth for a reason.*

*D*ear Gift Recipient,

I hope you realize the gift and power of your story. By reading, answering questions, and completing the exercises in this book, you've taken the foundational steps from reader to knower. You opened the gift of knowing who you are—knowing what feeds your soul and knowing why.

I intended this book to be a quick read. I wanted you to spend your time engaging in all things "you," whether it's an activity that brings you joy or it's a journaled thought or moment of stillness that reinforces the connection to your inner voice and authenticity.

Remember, your unique qualities separate you from everyone else; those qualities are your greatness. I hope you will continue to learn, discover, and never lose sight of who you are. There is only one you, and that makes you special.

All the best,
Joselyn

About the Author

Joselyn is passionate about helping people discover their unique qualities and the power of their life story. She used her creative superpowers to transform the emotional abuse she suffered as child into a purposeful, gratitude-filled adulthood. Joselyn now guides readers on their own journey of self-discovery to find their greatness and live with personal authenticity. She designs and facilitates workshops that help participants attain personal fulfillment, recognize the importance of self-care, and live their best life. To find out more about Joselyn, visit https://joselynsmithgreene.com.

Acknowledgments

To all the cheerleaders I've met along the way who inspired, and contributed to my self-discovery journey, I thank you. You helped reshape, redefine, and recreate who I am and how I see myself. Know that your words, acknowledgments, and gestures are truly a gift that keeps on giving.

To my husband, Glen: Thank you for being the quintessential cheerleader, who is always ready and supportive of my next big idea. That says a lot, since I've had many. To my sons: Justin and Evan, you are the reason I will always strive to be emotionally whole. My intent is to leave you a legacy that champions your own happiness and greatness. I hope you will pass it on. To my mother: You supported and encouraged my quest to stand in my truth and welcomed our "below the surface" conversations. To my sister, Barbara: Our marathon conversations helped me immensely in my struggle to heal. You lifted me up more times than I can count. To my brother, Hume: Thank you for sharing your experience growing up. I gained a broader prospective of what was.

To my editor, Marla Markman: A special thank you for providing me with honest, gentle feedback without breaking my spirit. It's been a valuable learning experience, and I'm glad I listened.

Made in the USA
Columbia, SC
25 February 2021